Illustrations by Shiela Marie Alejandro

Visit her website: https://www.bucketsofwhimsies.com

Shirley St. Publishing and the Adventures of Stella and Roman are trademarks of Shirley St. Publishing. Winthrop, MA.

Summary: The day in the life of two children in Winthrop, MA in the Summer of 2016

ISBN-13: 978-0-9988007-0-7
Printed in the U.S.A.

Stella & Roman,

I hope that your children and your childrens, children read this book one day. Be sure they can feel our families love and smell the ocean. We could have lived these days for the rest of our life.

Mom and Dad

**Breakfast together is how we start our day,
brush our teeth, put on our swimsuits and fly away.**

Sea worms are scary and will bite you if you don't watch out.
We keep them in a box so they can hideout.

I put the card in the gate with a forward motion.
it's time to sail, fish, and swim in the ocean!

WINTHROP
ELKS
CLUB

Our dinghy will get us to our sail boat named "Go Bucks". I'll bring some bread to feed the ducks.

Seeing the other boats in the Winthrop cove is so exciting.
I keep my eyes peeled for a seal or jellyfish sighting.

I need my goggles before I jump off the boat.
The life vest keeps me afloat.

Fishing off the boat is so much fun.
Since it's almost lunchtime, we are done.

Lunch Time **!** Hotdogs, macaroni and cheese gives us energy
and fills our tummy. The food at the Winthrop Yacht Club
is just so yummy.

Driving the dinghy back to the Elks is the best.
Before we head back to the boat, we have to put on our life vest.

To help feed our friends with our charity, we go to
the Arbors and pick up food. Joannie and Lorie are
so kind and put us in the best mood.

Delivering food to those in need is an honor and wonderful opportunity.

Mi Amore is how we serve our community.

The Sisters are always so kind and full of joy.
Every time I leave their house, I have a new toy.

The night is over and it's time to read Fancy Nancy and The Noon Balloon. On this warm summer night, we look out the window at the bright and shiny moon.

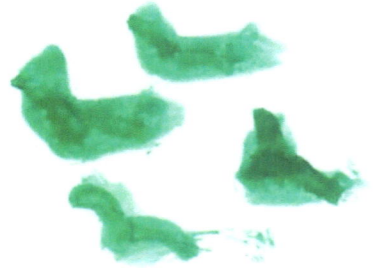

Roman

3/5/2017

Stella

3/5/2017

The End...☺

www.ingramcontent.com/pod-product-compliance
Lightning Source LLC
Chambersburg PA
CBHW042120040426
42449CB00002B/115